LEAD
Guitar

Steve MacKay

Published by Hinkler Books Pty Ltd
45–55 Fairchild Street
Heatherton Victoria 3202 Australia
www.hinkler.com.au

hinkler

© Hinkler Books Pty Ltd 2011

Author: Steve MacKay
Cover Design: Sam Grimmer
Prepress: Graphic Print Group
Typesetting: MPS Limited
Photography: Ned Meldrum Digital
Amplifier © Shutterstock/Ronald Sumners

ISBN: 978 1 7418 5806 8

Printed and bound in China

Contents

Introduction

The aim of this book is to get you improvising as quickly as possible while providing guidance towards a deeper understanding of *how* improvising actually works.

The definition of 'improvising' or 'soloing' is spontaneous musical creation – music performed without preparation. Yet every time you hear a musician 'improvise', they are playing phrases and musical concepts within a 'context' – improvisation is the spontaneous arrangement of established ideas and musical concepts.

An analogy would be speaking or communicating. When we speak, we are not saying words we have never spoken before, but we are creating sentences with words we already know in order to express ourselves. When we are young we learn how to speak, we learn words and their meanings, and then we spontaneously put all of that information together to communicate.

I have identified a common problem: guitarists often learn one scale (usually the blues scale) and then expect it to sound good when they play it over anything and everything. This is the equivalent of learning a few words and expecting them to express everything you need to say within any context.

This book is my attempt at a simple solution to this problem.

Essential Theory

Glossary

The hardest part of learning anything new is familiarising yourself with, and understanding, all of the terms and expressions.

This section is designed to be your 'go to' for any terms or words you may not be familiar with. If I have failed to include something and you are scratching your head about it, try searching for it on the internet.

The guitar neck

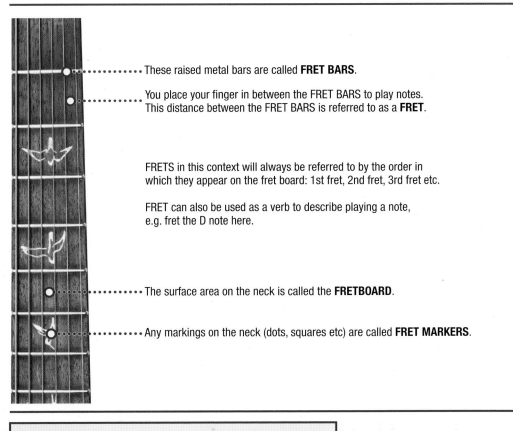

These raised metal bars are called **FRET BARS**.

You place your finger in between the FRET BARS to play notes. This distance between the FRET BARS is referred to as a **FRET**.

FRETS in this context will always be referred to by the order in which they appear on the fret board: 1st fret, 2nd fret, 3rd fret etc.

FRET can also be used as a verb to describe playing a note, e.g. fret the D note here.

The surface area on the neck is called the **FRETBOARD**.

Any markings on the neck (dots, squares etc) are called **FRET MARKERS**.

If you don't know the string names, how to find notes all over the neck, what position playing is, how chords are formed and other basics, I recommend reading my first book, *Simply Guitar*, which covers all these points in detail.

Tab symbols

Here are the tab symbols you will come across in this book. I will provide a brief description of what each symbol means in relation to the tabbed notes in the example illustration.

Slide down

Pick the note on the 5th fret and, while maintaining the pressure applied by your fretting finger, slide the note down to the 3rd fret without picking and without releasing any pressure by your fretting finger.

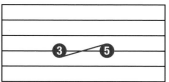

Slide up

Pick the note on the 3rd fret and, while maintaining the pressure applied by your fretting finger, slide the note up to the 5th fret without picking and without releasing any pressure by your fretting finger.

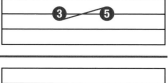

Hammer on

Pick the note on the 3rd fret and, while maintaining the pressure applied by your first finger, put your third finger on the 5th fret in a 'hammer' type action without picking.

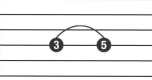

Pull off

Place your first finger on the 3rd fret and your third finger on the 5th fret. Pick the note on the 5th fret, then 'pull off' your third finger in a plucking-type action, essentially playing the note held by your first finger.

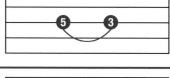

Half step bend

Pick the note on the 3rd fret with your 3rd finger and using your first, second and third fingers bend the string upwards on the fret board until you raise the tension by a semitone.

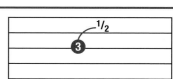

Whole step bend

Pick the note on the 3rd fret with your 3rd finger and using your first, second and third fingers bend the string upwards on the fret board until you raise the tension by a tone. (This can be very difficult on an acoustic guitar.)

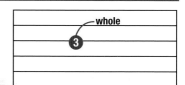

Chord shapes

Chord shapes are shown with simple diagrams indicating where to place your fingers on the fret board to form a particular chord.

0 means play that string OPEN (with no fingers fretting any notes).

X means do not play that string.

The numbers tell you which fingers on your fretting hand are used.

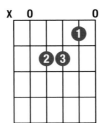

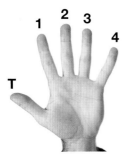

Here is the guitar neck from a frontal perspective.

Here is the chord shape above placed on the guitar neck, indicating where your fingers go.

Scale diagrams

Scale diagrams show the guitar neck from your playing perspective.

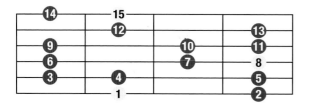

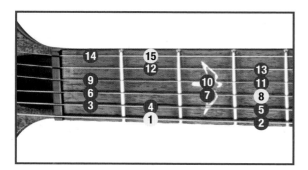

You can think of scale diagrams as an image of the guitar neck as though you had the guitar sitting flat on your lap facing upwards:

- The horizontal lines represent the strings.
- The vertical lines represent the frets.
- The circles represent where the notes of the scale appear on the fret board.
- The numbers within the circles tell you which order to play the notes.
- The light circles tell you where the 'root notes' are.

The 'root note' in a scale or a chord indicates the starting note, that is, the note that denotes which key you are in. For example, the root note of a C blues scale will be C. The root note of a D major chord will be D.

Position playing

Unlike chord shapes (also known as diagrams), the numbers on the diagrams below tell you in which order to play the notes, not which finger to use. To know which finger to use we implement position playing.

First position would be first finger on the 1st fret, second finger on the 2nd fret, third finger on the 3rd fret and fourth finger on the 4th fret.

Fifth position would be first finger on the 5th fret, second finger on the 6th fret, third finger on the 7th fret and fourth finger on the 8th fret.

first position

fifth position

How to read tablature (TAB)

Tablature, or tab as it is commonly referred to, was around long before music notation was invented – some say it originated in China over 30,000 years ago. Tab is a very convenient way to depict how to play notes and chords on the guitar.

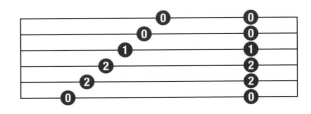

In the above diagram:

- The lines represent the strings.
- The numbers tell you which fret to play (remember, O means OPEN string).
- When the numbers are stacked on top of each other, they show a chord.

What you need to know about chords

Chords are three or more notes played simultaneously. That means technically you could play three different notes at once on a piano or a guitar and you would be playing a chord – whether or not it would sound good is another story!

All chords are created from three or more notes derived from the major scale. To really understand the structure of chords, you must first understand the major scale. An analogy for this might be: you wouldn't build a house without first knowing the architectural plans.

Right now you need to know the following:

- Chords are created from three or more notes derived from the major scale. These notes are arranged into formulas or, as I like to think of them, 'recipes'.
- You can break chords up into three main groups: major, minor and dominant.

These three chord groups have their own distinct sounds, much like flavours have their own distinct tastes. To have sweet you would use sugar, to have savoury you would use salt and to have sour you would use something acidic, like vinegar.

Chords are the same: to have major chords you use the 1st, 3rd and 5th notes of the major scale (Formula = 1, 3, 5), *creating a 'happy' sound.*

To have minor chords you use the 1st, flattened 3rd and 5th notes of the major scale (Formula = 1, $\flat$3, 5), *creating a 'sad' sound.*

To have dominant chords you use the 1st, 3rd, 5th and flattened 7th notes of the major scale (Formula = 1, 3, 5, $\flat$7), *creating a 'bluesy' sound.*

> You may be wondering what a flattened 3rd is. Put your finger on the 5th fret of the high E string. This note is A. Move up one fret and the note becomes A sharp (A$\sharp$), that is, you have 'sharpened' the note by moving it up one fret. Now go back to the A note (A natural). Now move back one fret. You are now playing A flat (A$\flat$), that is, you have 'flattened' the note by moving back a fret.

A$\flat$	A	A$\sharp$
flat	natural	sharp
←		→

major	1	3	5	
minor	1	$\flat$3	5	
dominant	1	3	5	$\flat$7

All chords are extensions or variations of these three basic chord formulas. I will include formulas with all of the chords mentioned in this book. Even if you don't fully understand them yet, try to remember what they are.

What you need to know about scales

Like chords, scales are also referenced from the major scale. Here are all of the notes in Western music (the musical alphabet):

A	A♯	B	C	C♯	D	D♯	E	F	F♯	G	G♯

After G♯ you end up back at A, only an octave higher in pitch. What is an octave? Sing the intro riff of the song 'My Sharona' by The Knack or the opening two notes of 'Somewhere over the Rainbow'. These notes are the same but one is higher in pitch – that is an octave. (There is a more theoretical explanation, but I'll get to that later – see page 17.)

To relate this to guitar, play the low E string open and then count up through the musical alphabet until you reach the 12th fret. Every note on the 12th fret is exactly one octave higher than the open strings.

Before I elaborate on this, there are a couple of terms you need to know: tones and semitones.

Tones and semitones both describe distance between one note and the next, for example, moving one tone up from A will give you B:

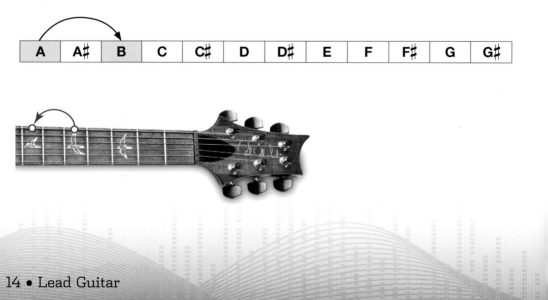

Moving one tone up from C♯ will give you D♯:

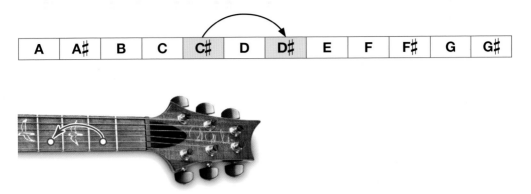

A	A♯	B	C	C♯	D	D♯	E	F	F♯	G	G♯

Moving one semitone up from B will give you C:

A	A♯	B	C	C♯	D	D♯	E	F	F♯	G	G♯

Moving one semitone up from D will give you D♯:

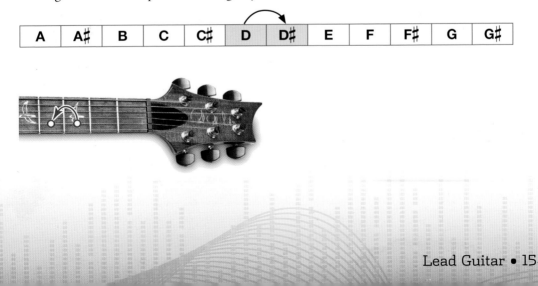

A	A♯	B	C	C♯	D	D♯	E	F	F♯	G	G♯

On guitar this is even easier:

- To move up a tone, just move up 2 frets.

- To move up a semitone, just move up 1 fret.

> The other name for a tone is a 'whole step'.
>
> The other name for a semitone is 'half step'.

Now that you know about tones (whole steps) and semitones (half steps) I can explain how scale formulas work.

The major scale is like the mother ship. Everything is derived and referenced from it. The formula for a major scale looks like this:

Tone, Tone, Semitone, Tone, Tone, Tone, Semitone.

I will colour the notes that fall on the formula starting from A using the musical alphabet:

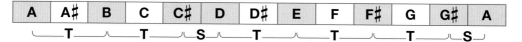

In this case, the scale would be A major because the formula was started on an A note.

Relating this back to guitar, starting from the open A string and moving up, the Tone, Tone, Semitone, Tone, Tone, Tone, Semitone formula would look like this:

A little more on chords

Here are the notes of the A major scale:

A	B	C♯	D	E	F♯	G♯	A
1	2	3	4	5	6	7	8

I have numbered each note to show you how chord formulas relate to the major scale.

The notes in an A major chord would be: A, C♯, E (1, 3, 5):

A	B	C♯	D	E	F♯	G♯	A
1	2	3	4	5	6	7	8

The notes in an A minor chord would be: A, C, E (1, ♭3, 5):

A	B	C	D	E	F♯	G♯	A
1	2	♭3	4	5	6	7	8

Notice how the C♯ becomes a C because of the ♭3rd (flattened 3rd).

More on octaves

Earlier I suggested you sing the opening line from 'My Sharona' or 'Somewhere over the Rainbow' to hear an octave. Now I can explain what an octave is in more detail.

Oct = 8, for example, an octopus has eight tentacles and an octagon has eight sides. An octave, then, is the 8th note of a major scale played against or simultaneously with the 1st note of the major scale.

A common abbreviation of the major scale formula is: T, T, S, T, T, T, S (T = Tone, S = Semitone).

Let's start the formula on a D note in the musical alphabet:

D	D♯	E	F	F♯	G	G♯	A	A♯	B	C	C♯	D

T — T — S — T — T — T — S

In this case, the scale would be D major because the formula was started on a D note.

These past few pages have had a lot of information to take in, but these are important topics to cover in order to understand the explanations of the fun stuff we are heading towards.

> **Note:** When abbreviated, 'minor' is always written with a lower case 'm'. Major is always abbreviated as an upper case M.

Basic Rock Improvisation

The 12 Bar Blues in the key of A – version 1

The 12 Bar Blues is a chord progression, 12 bars in length.

A chord progression is a series of chords that sound good together and 'progress' towards a sound of 'resolution'.

A 'bar' refers to music notation. One bar of music usually contains 4 beats, for example, '1, 2, 3, 4'.

I am going to show you two versions of the 12 Bar Blues, both in the key of A. Version 1 has a very simple harmony (only two notes at a time). Version 2 has chords (three or more notes at a time) – we will look at this later in the 'More Complex Improvisation' section.

Here is version 1:

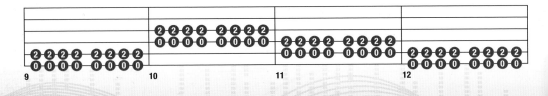

Two shapes of the A blues scale

The blues scale is very similar to another scale called the minor pentatonic scale. Pentatonic scales contain just 5 notes (pentagram = 5 points, pentagon = 5 sides).

Blues scales are identical to minor pentatonic scales except for the addition of a flattened 5th note (the blues note), making the blues scale a 6 note scale.

There are five shapes of the pentatonic and blues scales. These shapes are also referred to as 'patterns'. Every shape contains exactly the same notes; they just appear in different places depending on what position you are playing in.

We are going to learn two of the most commonly used blues scale shapes.

Shape 1

Play the first scale shape starting on the 5th fret.

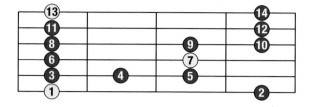

Shape 2

The second shape starts on the 2nd note of the first scale shape (starting on the 8th fret).

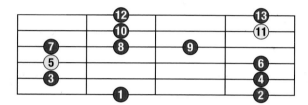

These two scale shapes are 'moveable' shapes that can be played anywhere on the neck. I have coloured the root notes lighter to help you identify where you would move them relative to the key you are playing in.

Start improvising!

Record yourself slowly playing the 12 Bar Blues in the key of A.

Practise playing the two blues scale shapes (as written on page 21) over the top of the recorded 12 Bar Blues in A.

Practise playing this scale forwards and backwards in a constant and consistent rhythm over the 12 Bar Blues.

When you start to feel confident with the scale, start exploring what you can do with it creatively. Notice what sounds good and what sounds bad. Explore and exhaust your options as this scale is going to be your friend for a long time!

> **Tip:** Try incorporating hammer ons, pull offs, bends and slides into your improvisation to add more expression.

What are licks?

In improvisation, a lick is similar to a quote or saying in speech, that is, an established concept that you apply to relevant circumstances when they arise.

Think about the main guitar riff in the song 'Johnny B Good'. This riff is a short melodic idea that is dynamic, has impact and can be reused over and over. This is referred to as a 'lick'.

This and the following entry include a selection of 18 popular licks to memorise that are useable over the 12 Bar Blues. Each lick is derived from the two blues scale shapes you have already learnt. (Note: You may encounter a note here and there that is not directly found in the 6 note blues scale.)

Try to be creative with mixing and matching them together.

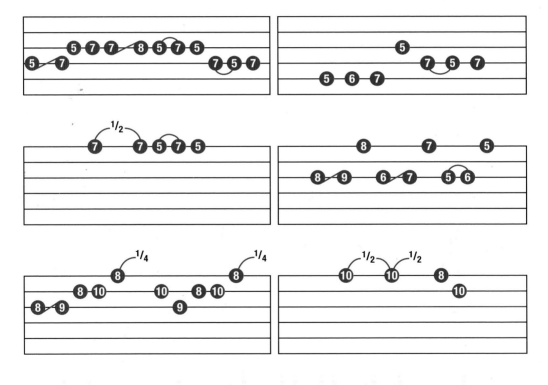

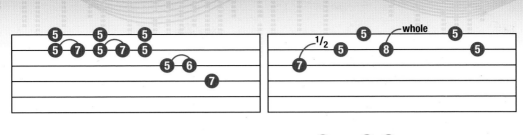

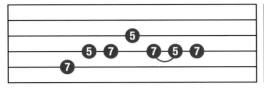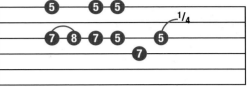

More licks

All of these licks are moveable (that is, they can be played in other keys), but for the purposes of this book I have written them in the key of A.

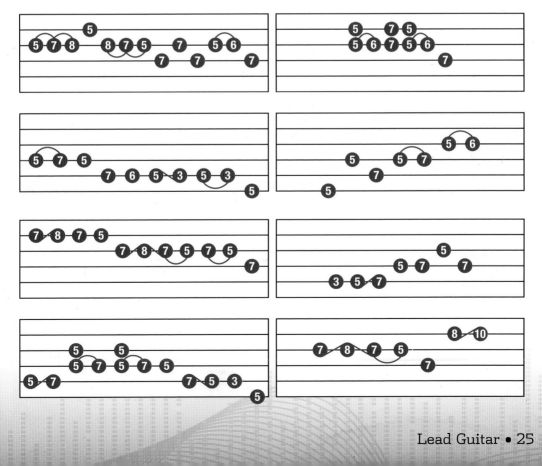

More Complex Improvisation

More on chord structure

The great thing about improvising over version 1 of the 12 Bar Blues is that you can get away with playing just the blues scale patterns and a few licks over the whole progression and sound pretty good!

This is possible because of the simple harmony of the 'power chords' you are improvising over.

A power chord is another name for a 5th interval being played in a chord-like fashion.

A 5th interval is simply the 1st and the 5th notes of the major scale. Refer to page 13 and see the chord formulas for major, minor and dominant 7th. The consistent ingredients in these chords are the 1 and the 5. This interval is called a 5th or a 'perfect 5th' because the sound is so resolved and complete. Think of the opening two notes from the *Star Wars* theme; this is an example of a 5th interval – very powerful!

As discussed previously, a basic chord is made up of three notes. This basic chord is called a triad (tri = 3 – think tripod, trimester, triangle etc).

Here are the major and minor triad formulas that we learnt on page 13:

major	1	3	5
minor	1	♭3	5

Notice that the difference between a major and a minor chord is dependent on whether the 3rd is natural or flattened. A natural 3rd will make the chord sound happy while a flattened 3rd will make the chord sound sad.

The word 'harmony' derives from a Greek word roughly meaning 'in agreement' or 'in balance'. In music, harmony relates to two or more notes being played simultaneously or against each other.

Next we have the most common 7th chord formulas:

major 7	1	3	5	7
dominant 7	1	3	5	♭7
minor 7	1	♭3	5	♭7

We now know that the difference between a major and minor chord is whether the 3rd is flattened or not, and that this affects the overall sound or mood of the chord. Observe the difference between a major7 chord and a dominant 7th chord. The 7th is flattened in a dominant 7th chord.

The sound difference between a major7 and a dominant7 is also quite substantial. The major 7th chord sound is used in a lot of lounge music. Think of the first chord in 'Girl from Ipanema' – it's very smooth sounding. The dominant 7th chord has a more funky sound and is used extensively across all popular genres of music.

In summary:

The 1st tells you what the root of the chord is.
The 3rd determines whether the chord is happy or sad.
The 5th adds foundation to the 1st.
The 7th determines whether the chord is smooth sounding or funky.

To fully understand all of this I always imagine a house:
The 1st is the location of the house.
The 3rd is who lives there – a happy person or a sad person.
The 5th is the bricks and mortar.
The 7th is how the house is decorated – retro smooth or funky shagpile!

Extensions

Next we have the most common 'extensions' for major chords. Extensions are the notes that are added after a 7th (they always appear in this order = 9, 11, 13).

To avoid confusion, I'll show you how the numbering of extensions works. I will use the C major scale as an example.

C	D	E	F	G	A	B	C
1	2	3	4	5	6	7	8/1

You can see that C is the first note, D is the second note, E is the third note and so on.

Extensions are made from the notes of the major scale only up the second octave and numbered sequentially.

C	D	E	F	G	A	B	C	D	E	F	G	A	B	C
1	2	3	4	5	6	7	8/1	9/2	10/3	11/4	12/5	13/6	14/7	15/1

You will notice how the 9th is the same note as the 2nd, the 11th is the same as the 4th and the 13th is the same as the 6th.

C	D	E	F	G	A	B	C	D	E	F	G	A	B	C
1	2	3	4	5	6	7	8/1	9/2	10/3	11/4	12/5	13/6	14/7	15/1

The 2, 4 and 6 might be the same notes as the 9, 11 and 13, but they are an octave lower in pitch and very close to the notes used in a triad (1, 3, 5). The pitch of a note is very important to how it affects the sound of a chord.

C	D	E	F	G	A	B	C	D	E	F	G	A	B	C
1	2	3	4	5	6	7	8/1	9/2	10/3	11/4	12/5	13/6	14/7	15/1

Imagine a crowded room full of people talking. There are a lot of people talking at the pitches of 1, 3, 5 and 7. Now imagine one person speaking at the pitch of a 2. They will be drowned out by those talking at 1 and 3 because these pitches are so close to each other. Now if the 2 was an octave higher (i.e. a 9), their voice would cut through a lot more easily because there is nothing blocking that frequency.

					extensions		
major 9th	1	3	5	7	9		
major 11th	1	3	5	7	9	11	
major 13th	1	3	5	7	9	11	13

Here are the most common extensions for dominant chords:

					extensions		
dominant 9th	1	3	5	♭7	9		
dominant 11th	1	3	5	♭7	9	11	
dominant 13th	1	3	5	♭7	9	11	13

The most common extensions for minor chords:

					extensions		
minor 9th	1	♭3	5	♭7	9		
minor 11th	1	♭3	5	♭7	9	11	
minor 13th	1	♭3	5	♭7	9	11	13

Observe how the only changes to the structure of these chords lies on either the 3rd or the 7th.

Also notice how in all minor chords, the 3rd and 7th notes are flattened. The only time the 7th is not flattened is when it is specifically a major7 chord.

You might be thinking a minor13 or a major13 chord has seven notes in it, yet you have only four fingers and there are only six strings!

This is where thinking of a chord as a house comes in handy. In any 13th chord (major, dominant or minor) you can generally omit the following:

- The 5th – the foundation is already being covered by the 1st.
- The 9th and 11th – the 13th is the one we want to hear.

We always need to keep:

- The 1st – this tells us where the house is.
- The 3rd – this tells us whether who lives in the house is happy or sad.
- The 7th – this tells us the vibe of the house.
- The 13th – this is the added feature to enhance the vibe of the house.

This same rule applies with the 9th and 11th – these notes are just additional features to enhance the vibe of the house.

All chords can be substituted by other chords within the same family. Here are a few examples:

Major family

Major chords can be substituted with major7th chords.

Major7th chords can be substituted with major9th chords.

Major9th chords can be substituted with major11th chords.

Major11th chords can be substituted with major13th chords.

(or any combination of)

Dominant 7th family

7th chords can be substituted for 9th chords.

9th chords can be substituted for 11th chords.

11th chords can be substituted for 13th chords.

(or any combination of)

Minor family

Minor chords can be substituted with minor7th chords.

Minor7th chords can be substituted with minor9th chords.

Minor9th chords can be substituted with minor11th chords.

Minor11th chords can be substituted with minor13th chords.

(or any combination of)

The 12 Bar Blues in the key of A – version 2 (chords)

These chord shapes can be played anywhere on the neck. The first note (root) will give the chord its name.

Dom7 Chord (dominant 7th)

Root note on the E string

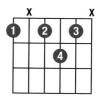

Formula: 1, 3, 5, ♭7

9 Chord (dominant 9th)

Root note on the A string

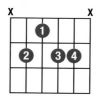

Formula: 1, 3, 5, ♭7, 9

The following diagrams show *where* to play each of these chords in order to play the 12 Bar Blues in A:

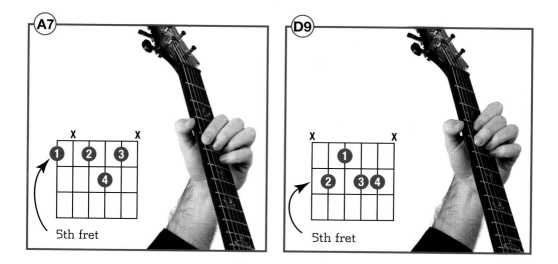

A7

5th fret

D9

5th fret

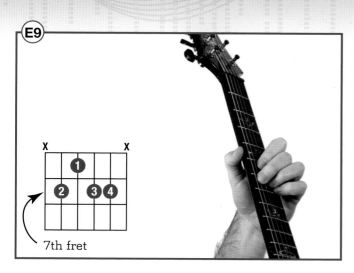

E9

X   X

7th fret

Here is the order in which you play these chords for the 12 Bar Blues:

A7	D9	A7	A7
1	2	3	4

D9	D9	A7	A7
5	6	7	8

E9	D9	A7	E9
9	10	11	12

Each block represents a bar of music, which has four counts. In other words, you strum each chord four times within the bar.

A7	D9	A7	A7
////	////	////	////

D9	D9	A7	A7
////	////	////	////

E9	D9	A7	E9
////	////	////	////

When you become used to playing the 12 Bar Blues chord progression, you will start to recognise many songs that use this chord progression, especially rock and roll from the 1950s onwards (from Elvis to ACDC).

If you find the moveable chord shapes too difficult, here are some non-moveable simple shapes, which are easier ways to play the chords needed for the A 12 Bar Blues:

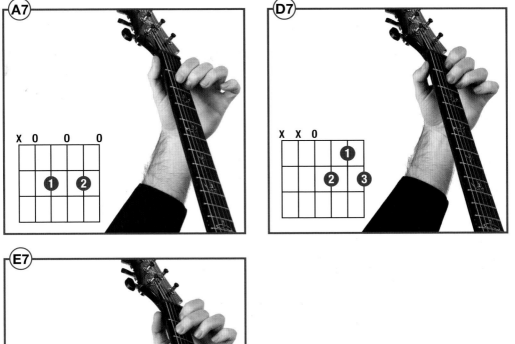

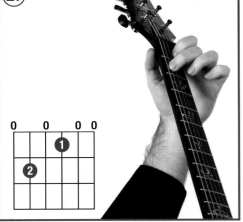

Notice that instead of D9 and E9, I have written D7 and E7.

D9 can be substituted for D7 and vice versa. An extended version of a 7th chord is a 9th chord and the two can be substituted for each other.

7th chord formula: 1, 3, 5, $\flat$7
9th chord formula: 1, 3, 5, $\flat$7, 9

Nuts and bolts of improvisation

In this book I am only going to explore the 12 Bar Blues in the key of A, but my aim is to provide you with the tools to take things a lot further on your own. By understanding the mechanics of improvising over chords, you won't be limited by anything you have rote learnt.

Unlike the power chords or 5th chords used in version 1 of the 12 Bar Blues, version 2 of the 12 Bar Blues has chords with more complex harmony. The notes that make up the chords require special attention when you are improvising over them. If you have wondered why sometimes the blues scale works over songs and sometimes it doesn't . . . here's why!

Let's break apart each chord and compare it to the A blues scale we used earlier. The A blues scale has these notes:

A	A♯	B	C	C♯	D	D♯	E	F	F♯	G	G♯
1			♭3		4	♭5	5			♭7	

An 'A7' chord has these notes:

A	A♯	B	C	C♯	D	D♯	E	F	F♯	G	G♯
1				3			5			♭7	

The notes I have coloured *green* in the A blues scale will clash with the notes in the A7 chord:

A	A♯	B	C	C♯	D	D♯	E	F	F♯	G	G♯
1			♭3		4	♭5	5			♭7	

The C note in the blues scale will clash with the C♯ note in the A7 chord because it is the 3rd of the chord, and as we have learnt, the 3rd is a *very* important ingredient in defining the sound of any chord.

The A7 has a happy-sounding 3rd and the blues scale has a sad ♭3rd. This conflict creates an 'off' sounding note in the scale akin to when a singer sings a bung note.

> The D♯ note I have coloured *orange* is considered the 'blues note' or 'blue note', which technically clashes a lot of the time anyway — its purpose is to create tension, which can sound really cool. Treat this note like a hot coal — you don't hold it too long!

Here is the same comparison with the A blues scale and the D7 chord.

A blues scale:

A	A♯	B	C	C♯	D	D♯	E	F	F♯	G	G♯
1			♭3		4	♭5	5			♭7	

D7 chord:

D	D♯	E	F	F♯	G	G♯	A	A♯	B	C	C♯
1				3			5			♭7	

The A blues scale does not contain the 3rd of the D7 chord. This isn't so much a clash as it is an important ingredient missing.

Here is the same comparison with the A blues scale and the E7 chord.

A blues scale:

A	A♯	B	C	C♯	D	D♯	E	F	F♯	G	G♯
1			♭3		4	♭5	5			♭7	

E7 chord:

E	F	F♯	G	G♯	A	A♯	B	C	C♯	D	D♯
1				3			5			♭7	

This time there is a G note in the A blues scale and the 3rd note of the E7 chord is a G♯. When one 3rd and another 3rd clash, it's like a personality clash and that always ends up being no good!

Now I have pointed out the problems, it's time for some solutions!

What scale over which chord?

The previous pages of this book have all been leading to this point. The information you are about to read will help you understand the mechanics of scales and their relationship to chords in a way that should allow you to explore improvisation on your own.

We have established that the A blues scale will not work perfectly over all of the chords in the A 12 Bar Blues. Unfortunately, there is no magical scale at all that will work perfectly over any chord progression.

Here is one way I approach this dilemma. I've broken it down into seven steps:

1. Establish what key you are playing in: e.g. an A blues is in the key of A.

2. Write down the major scale notes of that key: e.g. A major.

3. Write down the major scale in two octaves that the chord you are improvising over is derived from: e.g. if playing over A7, write out the A major scale in two octaves. If playing over E7, write out the E major scale in two octaves.

4. Map out the notes of the chord you are improvising over in its full-extended form: e.g. E7 chord notes plus extensions – 1, 3, 5, ♭7, 9, 11, 13.

5. Compare the notes of the major scale of the key you are playing in (e.g. A major) with the notes from the chord you are improvising over (e.g. E7 and its extensions).

6. Arrange the notes of the chord you are improvising over in the same order as the major scale notes of the key you playing in (alphabetically).

7. Reconstruct the major scale of the key adding in the notes from the chord you are improvising over.

On the following pages we will go through this seven-step process with each chord in the A 12 Bar Blues.

> If you want to bypass the theory of *why* things are the way they are and just get on with learning scales that work over the chords in the A 12 Bar Blues, then go straight to the Cheat Sheet section on page 50.

What scale over A7?

Step 1: Establish what key you are playing in.

A, because we are playing an A 12 Bar Blues.

Step 2: Write down the major scale notes of that key.

To find the notes in the A major scale, write out the musical alphabet starting from A and colour the notes according to the formula for a major scale that we learnt about on page 16:

Tone, Tone, Semitone, Tone, Tone, Tone, Semitone = *major scale*

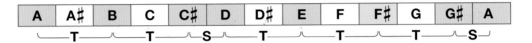

A	A♯	B	C	C♯	D	D♯	E	F	F♯	G	G♯	A
T		T		S		T		T		T		S

The notes of the A major scale are:

A	B	C♯	D	E	F♯	G♯	A
1	2	3	4	5	6	7	8

Step 3: Write down the major scale in two octaves that the chord you are playing over is derived from.

The A7 chord formula is derived from the A major scale so the notes are:

Changed

A	B	C♯	D	E	F♯	G	A	B	C♯	D	E	F♯	G
1	2	3	4	5	6	7	8	9	10	11	12	13	14

A major scale

1   3   5   ♭7   9   11   13

= 7t cord

Step 4: *Map out the notes of the chord you are playing over in its full-extended form.*

The formula for a 7th chord is:

1	3	5	b7

Extending a 7th chord out will give us:

1	3	5	b7	9	11	13

Therefore the notes are going to be:

A	B	C♯	D	E	F♯	G	A	B	C♯	D	E	F♯	G
1	2	3	4	5	6	b7	8	9	10	11	12	13	14

Notice I changed the 7th note of the A major scale which is a G♯, to a G to make it a b7 according to the formula of a 7th chord.

All of the notes belonging to A7 are:

A	C♯	E	G	B	D	F♯

chord = A7

Step 5: *Compare the notes of the A major scale with the notes from the A7 chord.*

The highlighted boxes show all of the chord extensions.

A major scale	A	B	C♯	D	E	F♯	G♯	A
interval	1	2	3	4	5	6	7	8

A7 chord	A	C♯	E	G	B	D	F♯
A7 formula	1	3	5	b7	9	11	13

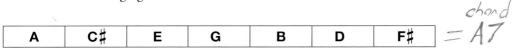

A7 chord   A B C♯ D E F♯ G
A7 formulat   1 9 3   11 5 13 b7

Reconstructed A B C♯ D E F♯ G A
               1 2 3   4 5 6   b7 8

Step 6: *Arrange the notes of the A7 chord in the same order as the A major scale (alphabetically).*

A7 chord	A	B	C♯	D	E	F♯	G
A7 formula	1	9	5	11	5	13	♭7

Step 7: *Reconstruct the A major scale adding in the notes from the A7 chord.*

reconstructed major scale	A	B	C♯	D	E	F♯	G	A
reconstructed major scale formula	1	2	3	4	5	6	♭7	8

I've highlighted the only difference between the A7 chord notes and the A major scale.

The scale to play over A7 is an A major scale with a ♭7.

formula	1	2	3	4	5	6	♭7	8

This formula gives us something called the Mixolydian mode. On page 47 we will learn what modes are and how they work. In the meantime, it is okay for you to know that a major scale with a ♭7 is called a Mixolydian mode.

Therefore, over A7 in the A 12 Bar Blues, you would use an A Mixolydian scale to improvise.

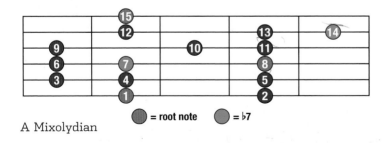

A Mixolydian

What scale over D7?

Step 1: *Establish what key you are playing in.*
We are playing an A 12 Bar Blues.

Step 2: *Write down the major scale notes of that key.*
The notes of the A major scale are:

A	B	C♯	D	E	F♯	G♯	A
1	2	3	4	5	6	7	8

Step 3: *Write down the major scale in two octaves that the chord you are playing over is derived from.*
The D7 chord formula is derived from the D major scale so the notes are:

D	D♯	E	F	F♯	G	G♯	A	A♯	B	C	C♯	D

T · T · S · T · T · T · S

D	E	F♯	G	A	B	C♯	D
1	2	3	4	5	6	7	8

D major scale

Step 4: *Map out the notes of the chord you are playing over in its full-extended form.*

The formula for a 7th chord is:

1	3	5	♭7

Extending a 7th chord out will give us:

1	3	5	♭7	9	11	13

To find the notes of a D7 chord fully extended, we need to map out the D major scale in two octaves then highlight the chord formula:

D	E	F♯	G	A	B	C	D	E	F♯	G	A	B	C♯
1	2	3	4	5	6	♭7	8	9	10	11	12	13	14

Notice I changed the 7th note of the D major scale which is a C♯ (see Figure 2), to a C to make it a ♭7 according to the formula of a 7th chord.

All of the notes belonging to D7 are:

D	F♯	A	C	E	G	B

Step 5: *Compare the notes of the A major scale with the notes from the D7 chord.*

The highlighted boxes show all of the chord's extensions.

A major scale	A	B	C♯	D	E	F♯	G♯	A
interval	1	2	3	4	5	6	7	8

D7 chord	D	F♯	A	C	E	G	B
D7 formula	1	3	5	♭7	9	11	13

A   B   C   D   E.FH.G
5   13   ♭7   1   9   6 ↑1

Step 6: *Arrange the notes of the D7 chord in the same order as the A major scale notes (alphabetically).*

D7 chord	A	B	C	D	E	F♯	G
D7 formula	5	13	♭7	1	9	3	11

Step 7: *Reconstruct the A major scale adding in the notes from the D7 chord.*

reconstructed major scale	A	B	C	D	E	F♯	G	A
reconstructed major scale formula	1	2	♭3	4	5	6	♭7	8

I've highlighted the only difference between the D7 chord notes and the A major scale.

The scale to play over D7 is an A major scale with a ♭3 and ♭7.

formula	1	2	♭3	4	5	6	♭7	8

This formula gives us the Dorian mode. Therefore, over D7 in the A 12 Bar Blues you would use an A Dorian mode to improvise.

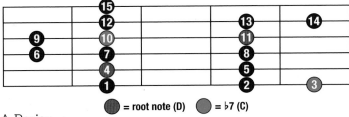

A Dorian

What scale over E7?

Step 1: *Establish what key you are playing in.*

A.

Step 2: *Write down the major scale notes of that key.*

The notes of the A major scale are:

A	B	C♯	D	E	F♯	G♯	A
1	2	3	4	5	6	7	8

Step 3: *Write down the major scale in two octaves that the chord you are playing over is derived from.*

The E7 chord formula is derived from the E major scale so the notes are:

E	F	F♯	G	G♯	A	A♯	B	C	C♯	D	D♯	E

T — T — S — T — T — T — S

E	F♯	G♯	A	B	C♯	D♯	E
1	2	3	4	5	6	7	8

E major scale

Step 4: *Map out the notes of the chord you are playing over in its full-extended form.*

The formula for a 7th chord is:

1	3	5	♭7

Extending a 7th chord out will give us:

1	3	5	♭7	9	11	13

To find the notes of an E7 chord fully extended, we need to map out the E major scale in two octaves, then highlight the chord formula:

E	F♯	G♯	A	B	C♯	D	E	F♯	G♯	A	B	C♯	D♯
1	2	3	4	5	6	♭7	8	9	10	11	12	13	14

Notice I changed the 7th note of the E major scale, which is a D♯ (see Figure 3), to a D to make it a ♭7 according to the formula of a 7th chord.

All of the notes belonging to E7 are:

E	G♯	B	D	F♯	A	C♯

Step 5: *Compare the notes of the A major scale with the notes from the E7 chord.*

The highlighted boxes show all of the chord's extensions.

A major scale	A	B	C♯	D	E	F♯	G♯	A
interval	1	2	3	4	5	6	7	8

E7 chord	E	G♯	B	D	F♯	A	C♯
E7 formula	1	3	5	♭7	9	11	13

Step 6: *Arrange the notes of the E7 chord in the same order as the A major scale notes (alphabetically).*

E7 chord	A	B	C♯	D	E	F♯	G♯
E7 formula	11	5	13	♭7	1	9	3

Step 7: *Reconstruct the A major scale adding in the notes from the E7 chord.*

reconstructed major scale	A	B	C♯	D	E	F♯	G♯	A
reconstructed major scale formula	1	2	3	4	5	6	7	8

The E7 chord notes are identical to the notes of the A major scale.

The scale to play over E7 is an A major scale.

formula	1	2	3	4	5	6	7	8

The major scale is also known as the Ionian mode. Therefore, over E7 in the A 12 Bar Blues you would use an A Ionian mode to improvise.

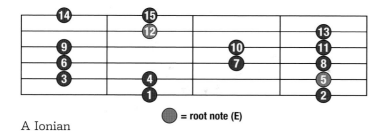

= root note (E)

A Ionian

What are modes?

People have written books on modes alone, so I will try to keep this explanation brief.

Modes are scales derived from the notes of the major scale. There are seven modes because a major scale has seven notes. Each mode plays through the major scale notes, only starting and finishing on a different degree. For example, here are the notes in the C major scale:

C	D	E	F	G	A	B
1	2	3	4	5	6	7

If I map out the notes of the C major scale starting on each degree, I will get the seven major modes:

Ionian	C	D	E	F	G	A	B
Dorian	D	E	F	G	A	B	C
Phrygian	E	F	G	A	B	C	D
Lydian	F	G	A	B	C	D	E
Mixolydian	G	A	B	C	D	E	F
Aeolian	A	B	C	D	E	F	G
Locrian	B	C	D	E	F	G	A

Here's the same thing, but I have coloured each note to make the pattern clearer:

Ionian	C	D	E	F	G	A	B
Dorian	D	E	F	G	A	B	C
Phrygian	E	F	G	A	B	C	D
Lydian	F	G	A	B	C	D	E
Mixolydian	G	A	B	C	D	E	F
Aeolian	A	B	C	D	E	F	G
Locrian	B	C	D	E	F	G	A

So you can see:

C	Ionian
D	Dorian
E	Phrygian
F	Lydian
G	Mixolydian
A	Aeolian
B	Locrian

The more you hear modes, the more you hear moods, much as minor chords sound sad and major chords sound happy. For example:

mode name	Ionian
formula	1, 2, 3, 4, 5, 6, 7
description	Sounds happy because it is exactly the same as the major scale. It also contains the notes needed to make all major chords.

mode name	Dorian
formula	1, 2, ♭3, 4, 5, 6, ♭7
description	To me, this sounds like a more sophisticated version of the pentatonic scale. Before I knew what Dorian was, I found I was already playing it. This mode articulates the sound of a minor 7th chord because it shares the same notes (1, ♭3, 5, ♭7).

mode name	Phrygian
formula	1, ♭2, ♭3, 4, 5, ♭6, ♭7
description	Has a very Spanish sound to it. Like the kind of mode Zorro would play if he was improvising! This is because of the tension created by the ♭2 and ♭6.

mode name	Lydian
formula	1, 2, 3, ♯4, 5, 6, 7
description	This sounds mystical to me, with a sort of 'wc sound. This mode is closely related to the major scale because it is virtually identical, but with a sharpened 4th.

mode name	Mixolydian
formula	1, 2, 3, 4, 5, 6, ♭7
description	Goes hand in hand with a dominant 7th chord because it shares the same notes (1, 3, 5, ♭7). It has a very 'rock and roll' sound to it.

mode name	Aeolian
formula	1, 2, ♭3, 4, 5, ♭6, ♭7
description	Sounds quite sad because it is exactly the same as the minor scale. Goes hand in hand with minor chords because it contains the 1, ♭3 and 5.

mode name	Locrian
formula	1, ♭2, ♭3, 4, ♭5, ♭6, ♭7
description	Has a certain impending doom sound to it. It relates well to diminished chords because it contains the 1, ♭3 and ♭5 notes used to build diminished chords. Diminished chords are the chords you hear played in black and white movies when someone is tied to the train tracks and a train is coming!

Modes are named after Greek islands and people. Making up your own way of identifying the character and colour of each mode is a great way to remember them.

Cheat sheet

This is the rote learning (memorisation by repetition) part of the book. I couldn't call myself a guitar teacher if I hadn't provided an explanation of *how* or *why* these scales work with 12 Bar Blues, but I also understand some people just want to play without getting too cerebral about it.

So for those who just want to dive in and improvise over the 12 Bar Blues in A, here is the information you need.

Use the A Mixolydian mode over the A7 chord:

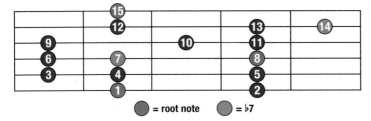

Use the A Dorian mode over the D7 or D9 chord:

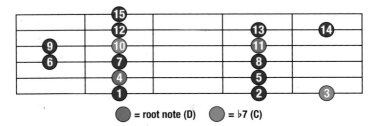

Use the A Ionian mode over the E7 or E9 chord:

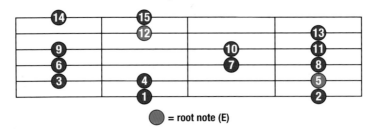

Try playing over just one chord at a time for a while so you get used to the mode shapes. Try to emphasise the root and ♭7 notes. Alternatively, you could use just the Mixolydian mode belonging to the root of each dom7 or 9th chord, for example, A Mixolydian over A7, D Mixolydian over D7, E Mixolydian over E7 and so on.

What are arpeggios?

The word 'arpeggio' comes from the Italian, meaning 'to spread a chord' – like how a harp is played.

On guitar, an arpeggio consists of notes from a chord played more like a scale; one note after the next either from the bottom upwards or the top downwards.

Consider that songs are made up of one or many 'chord progressions'. A chord progression is a series of chords that sound good together.

When improvising over a song made up of one or many chord progressions, playing the individual notes that make up the chords you are playing over will *always* sound correct. For this reason arpeggios are a great tool for any improviser's artillery ... and they sound cool.

Two moveable arpeggio shapes for the 12 Bar Blues

As discussed, this book features the popular rock and blues chord progression, the 12 Bar Blues. Here are the arpeggios for the chords used in the 12 Bar Blues.

Dominant 7th arpeggios

Position 1 (root note on the E string)

Formula:

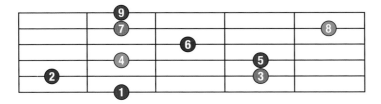

Position 2 (root note on the A string)

Formula: ① ③ ⑤ ♭7

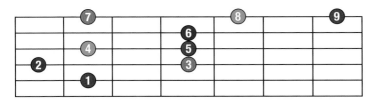

These arpeggios are moveable shapes, which means you can use them to play *every* dom7 arpeggio simply by moving them to the position on the neck relevant to the key you wish to play them in.

For example, if I wanted to play an Adom7 arpeggio, I would make the first note of the arpeggio shape I am playing an A. This could either be the 5th fret of the E string or the 12th fret of the A string depending on which arpeggio shape I want to play (position 1 or position 2).

> Dominant 7th chords and arpeggios are also just referred to as 7th and Dom7th.

Using arpeggios improvising over the 12 Bar Blues

Use the A7 arpeggio when the A7 chord is being played in the 12 Bar Blues:

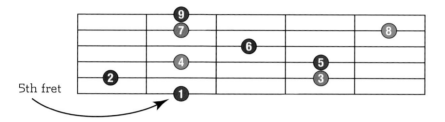

5th fret

Use the D7 arpeggio when the D9 chord is being played in the 12 Bar Blues:

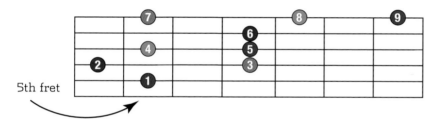

5th fret

Use the E7 arpeggio when the E9 chord is being played in the 12 Bar Blues:

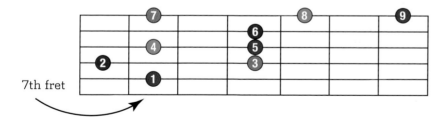

7th fret

> You can experiment with a combination of the modes we have learnt and these arpeggios. A good improviser often uses a combination of modes, licks and arpeggios.

Playing Techniques

How to practise scales in a useful way for improvising

Knowing how to play your scales forwards and backwards doesn't always mean you will be able to improvise easily with them. Improvising is not usually executed in such a linear way and if you try to play like that, it will most likely sound as though you are playing up and down a scale as opposed to improvising. To improvise a melody that isn't simply the notes of the scale, you need to skip notes, repeat notes, skip strings, and add expression and rhythm etc.

A good way to practise your scales is to turn the linear motion I referred to on its head. Try to challenge your knowledge of the scale pattern.

On the following pages I will include examples of the following techniques: sequencing notes, sequencing notes using intervals, consistent speed exercises, bending notes, sliding notes, vibrato and using octaves.

Sequencing notes

Sequencing means to arrange notes in a recurring, logical pattern. I will use the A major scale to demonstrate a typical sequencing pattern.

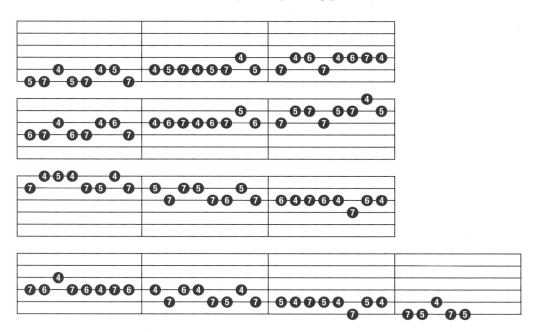

Sequencing notes using intervals

Playing through a scale and moving up by 3rds, 4ths, 5ths or 6ths can create a cool melodic effect. Find the patterns I've created with these sequences and apply them to any scale. These examples are in the key of A major.

3rds

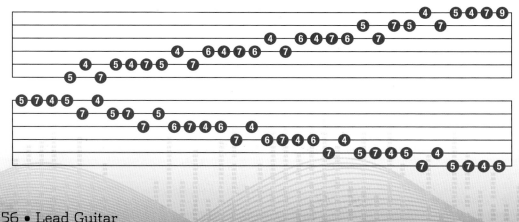

4ths

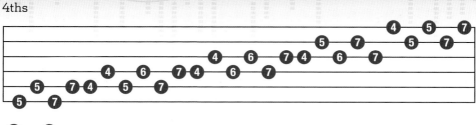

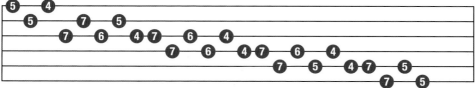

5ths

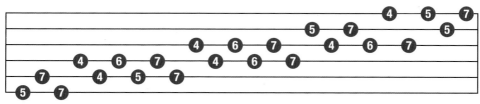

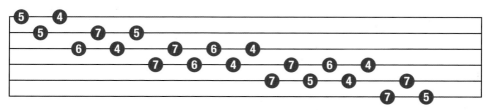

6ths

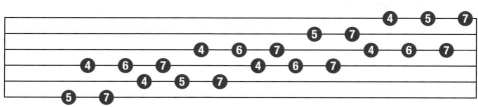

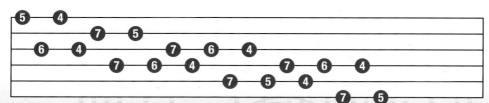

Consistent speed exercises – rhythm

As mentioned at the beginning of this section, improvising is not just about knowing your scale notes forwards and backwards – a lot of other important elements come into play. One of those elements is rhythm.

The best way to become good at rhythm is to practise it! There are four main rhythm exercises I will show you to get you started using the major scale.

Quarter notes

Each note is played on the count of 1, 2, 3, 4.

Eighth notes

Each note is played on the count of 1 &, 2 &, 3 &, 4 &. (You play notes on the '&' also.)

Sixteenth notes

Each note is played on the count of 1 e & a, 2 e & a, 3 e & a, 4 e & a. (You play notes on the 'e', '&' and 'a' also.)

Half an eighth is a sixteenth so the speed is exactly double of what it was with eighth notes.

Triplets

Each note is played on the count of 1 & a, 2 & a, 3 & a, 4 & a. (You play notes on the '&' and 'a' also.)

Triplets are 3 notes in the time of 2. Tap your foot in the same constant beat as before '1, 2, 3, 4, 1, 2, 3, 4' and so on. Now while you tap your foot say the word TRIP-A-LET, broken up into 3 syllables in each beat like so:

1			2			3			4		
trip	a	let	trip	a	let	trip	a	let	trip	a	let
1	&	a	2	&	a	3	&	a	4	&	a

It is a good idea to use a metronome to help you practise these rhythms with a solid reference for consistency. You can buy electric metronomes from any good music store or you can even download software metronomes from the internet.

Bending notes

Think of any rock guitar solo. That wailing sound is made by bending the strings or bending a single string. The idea is to push the string up on the guitar neck to raise the tension of the string, and this in turn raises the pitch. There is quite a degree of accuracy required to execute bending notes in a convincing way; that is, not sounding like a cat going crazy on the back fence.

There are two frequently used types of bends – 'half step' and 'whole step' bends. We learnt about half steps and whole steps on page 8.

Bending

1. A good way to practise bending notes up a half step is to pick a note on the guitar, for example, the D note on the high E string (10th fret).

2. Now play the note a half step up (D♯ on the 11th fret).

3. Now return to the original note (D on the 10th) and bend the note until it reaches the same pitch as the D♯. You only pick the note once, then bend it up.

This will take a bit of practise to nail correctly.

Repeat this process when practising whole step bends, but replace the half step with a whole step.

Sliding notes

Slides are another cool-sounding technique for guitar playing and improvising.

1. Play any note on the 3rd fret high E string (G).

2. Now keep your finger down the whole time and slide it up to the 5th fret of the high E string without releasing any tension.

You should hear the note sliding 'up'. You can slide forwards and backwards and to any note from anywhere.

Vibrato

Vibrato is achieved on guitar in two main ways:

1. Up and down (a very subtle version of a half step bend).

2. Side to side (like a violinist)

The aim is to create a pulsating-type effect in the way a vocalist or cellist does. This adds a lot of dimension, expression and feeling to your playing.

Using octaves

I am going to show you six commonly used movable octave shapes. As learnt on page 17, an octave is the 8th note of a major scale played against or simultaneously with the 1st note of the major scale.

When played simultaneously on guitar, this creates a thick, cool sound, as made famous by Charlie Christian, George Benson and many guitarists after them.

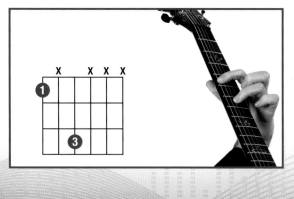

You can also use this shape on the A string.

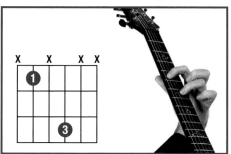

The shape changes when playing octaves on the D string.

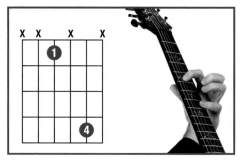

You can also use this shape on the G string.

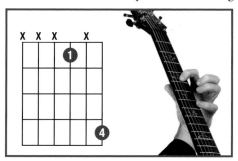

Then there are octave shapes using wider gaps between the strings.

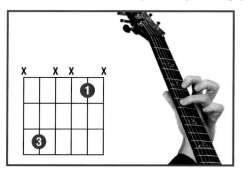

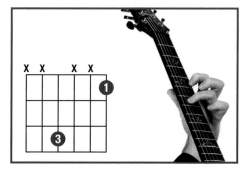

Here is the A major scale using these octave shapes:

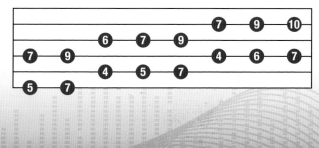

Conclusion

Music is a bit like quantum mechanics; the more you know, the more you realise you don't know! I say this not to be discouraging, but to point out that to be a musician is to be a student in perpetuity.

When I was approached to write a follow-up book to *Simply Guitar*, focusing on improvisation for beginners, I realised there are really two main categories of guitarists to which this applies:

1. Completely beginner guitarists who want to jump straight into improvisation.
2. Guitarists of varying levels who are beginners at improvisation.

This book is my attempt to provide information, instruction and answers for both profiles.

Improvising can be as simple as finger painting or as complex as an Escher drawing, so it was a challenge to identify what points to focus on. I sincerely hope this book has opened some doors for you and demystified some of that intimidating music theory that gets in the way of your progress.

Please drop into my website and stay posted for updates around some of the topics covered in this book: www.stevemackayguitar.com

Cheers,

Steve

About the Author

Steve Mackay is a highly accomplished musician, lead guitarist, music producer and guitar clinician. He is also a skilled guitar teacher and a best-selling author of guitar tuition books and DVDs.

In addition to teaching, Steve also regularly performs and records professionally. He has recorded and performed guitar in the USA, the UK, Europe and Australia, on high-profile radio and TV shows, on nationally televised music awards and on stage in front of thousands of people. This depth of practical knowledge and experience comes through in *Lead Guitar*.

Most importantly, Steve's most relevant skill is the ability to make it easy for others to learn what he knows. As a teacher, Steve demystifies the art of guitar performance into small chunks of information that are:

- easy to understand;
- easy to learn; and
- easy to implement.

Steve's simplified teaching techniques have resulted in his first guitar book, *Simply Guitar*, selling over 1 million copies globally and helping countless people learn to play the guitar with ease and enjoyment.